The Unseen Force

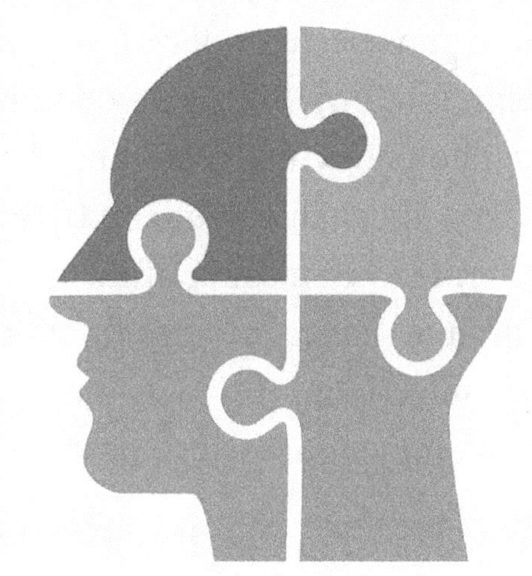

Harnessing the Hidden Power of Your
Subconscious Mind

Allan Miranda

Copyright © 2023 by Allan Miranda

This book is a work of nonfiction. The views and opinions expressed in this book are solely those of the author and do not necessarily reflect the official policy or position of any organization, company, or individual mentioned within.

Table of Contents

Introduction: Awakening the Hidden Potential

In a society filled with continual distractions and the chase of outward achievement, we frequently neglect one of the most formidable forces inside us: the subconscious mind. This mysterious region, buried under the surface of our conscious consciousness, contains the key to unleashing our full potential and reshaping our lives in astonishing ways.

Throughout history, countless civilizations and spiritual traditions have acknowledged the significant significance of the subconscious mind. From ancient techniques of meditation and visualization to current scientific investigations, there is a plethora of data that confirms the enormous power inherent inside us.

A recent scientific study in the area of neuroscience has uncovered remarkable insights into the workings of the human brain. Studies have proven that the subconscious mind is not only an idle spectator, but an active player in forming our ideas, emotions, actions, and eventually, our reality. It is a storehouse of boundless creativity, intuitive understanding, and tremendous healing qualities.

Consider the tales of people who have accomplished incredible accomplishments in the face of adversity. From athletes who exceed their own physical boundaries to entrepreneurs who realize their ambitions despite all circumstances, these people delve into the wellspring of their subconscious minds.

Moreover, improvements in brain imaging technology have shown the interconnection of our conscious and subconscious thoughts. The study demonstrates that our subconscious mind absorbs information at an incredible pace, making split-second judgments and impacting our behaviors even before we consciously recognize them. It is the driving force behind our behaviors, beliefs, and the consequences we draw into our life.

In this book, we will dig into the intriguing domain of the subconscious mind and examine practical strategies to harness its power. We will learn the techniques of meditation, visualization, and affirmations that have been practiced for millennia to unleash the latent potential inside. Drawing upon proven techniques and tactics, we will go on a journey to reprogram our belief systems, nurture positive thinking habits, and tap into our inner creativity.

Furthermore, we will learn how to coordinate our conscious and subconscious efforts toward reaching our objectives and desires. By understanding the immense significance of the subconscious mind, we may harness its influence to produce plenty, success, and pleasure in all parts of our life.

Prepare to go on a revolutionary trip as we explore the hidden possibilities inside your subconscious mind. By the conclusion of this book, you will possess the knowledge and skills to tap into this wellspring of power, transcend self-imposed boundaries, and build a life that is in accordance with your innermost wishes and ambitions. Get ready to uncover the secret energy inside you.

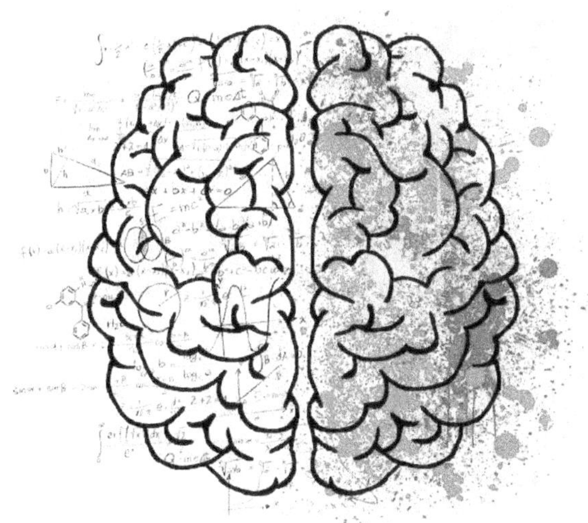

Chapter 1: The Subconscious Mind Unveiled

Understanding the Subconscious Mind

The human mind is a complex and multidimensional organism, comprising both conscious and subconscious parts. While our conscious mind rules our immediate awareness and rational reasoning, it is the subconscious mind that holds the key to unlocking our real potential. In this chapter, we will dig into the nature of the subconscious mind and study its enormous effect on our ideas, emotions, and actions.

The subconscious mind might be compared to the enormous depths of an ocean, brimming with hidden riches and unknown places. It functions discreetly, under the surface, but its influence reverberates throughout our lives. It is responsible for a myriad of activities, including storing memories, processing emotions, and controlling autonomic physical systems. However, its effect goes well beyond these everyday chores.

One of the most remarkable characteristics of the subconscious mind is its involvement in molding our world. Countless studies have proved that our ideas and beliefs, whether conscious or unconscious, have a direct influence on the results we encounter in life. The subconscious mind operates as a filter, selectively receiving and interpreting the information it receives depending on our internal training.

Consider a basic example: You wake up in the morning feeling unpleasant and anticipate your day to be filled with problems and hassles. As the day develops, you realize that your encounters actually mirror your negative expectations, validating your original assumption. What you may not understand is that your subconscious mind, driven by your underlying negative programming, has played a key part in attracting these situations.

On the other side, those who possess a positive outlook and an unshakeable conviction in their skills frequently actualize great results. This is not simply coincidence; it is the consequence of the subconscious mind connecting their thoughts, emotions, and actions with their intended results. By acknowledging the power of their subconscious mind and acting in sync with it, these people harness a force that drives them toward achievement.

The Role of the Subconscious in Shaping Reality

To appreciate the actual power of the subconscious mind, it is vital to acknowledge its role in molding our world.

The subconscious mind functions based on the notion of perception becoming reality. It does not discriminate between the exterior environment and our interior ideas and beliefs. Instead, it regards all information as genuine and acts upon it appropriately.

Imagine that you have a deep-rooted notion that you are not deserving of financial wealth. This notion, buried inside your subconscious mind, impacts your thoughts, emotions, and behaviors in subtle but powerful ways. As a consequence, you may find yourself unknowingly rejecting prospects for money, undermining financial attempts, or enduring a continual sensation of need.

However, by being aware of your subconscious programming and actively modifying it, you may change your reality. By replacing limiting ideas with powerful ones, you may reprogram your subconscious mind to attract riches, prosperity, and success. It is a process that demands patience, perseverance, and a profound commitment to personal progress.

In future chapters, we will examine numerous strategies and practices to tap into the power of your subconscious mind. We will go into the worlds of meditation, visualization, and affirmations, which serve as potent tools for reprogramming your subconscious. By learning to harness the secret energy inside, you will start on a path of self-discovery and change.

Prepare to unleash the untapped power of your subconscious mind as we travel the depths of its impact. Through this research, you will get a comprehensive knowledge of how your ideas, beliefs, and emotions affect your world. Together, we will begin a revolutionary adventure towards unlocking the actual potential of your subconscious mind.

Chapter 2: Tapping into the Subconscious Mind

Exploring Meditation and Visualization Techniques

The subconscious mind is a world of great power and untapped potential. To harness its talents, we must examine methods that allow us to access and interact with this hidden energy inside us. In this chapter, we will dig into two strong techniques: meditation and visualization.

Meditation has been practiced for generations as a technique of quieting the mind, fostering inner calm, and connecting with deeper elements of our awareness. Beyond its well-known advantages of stress reduction and relaxation, meditation provides a route to reaching the subconscious mind. By quieting the bustle of the conscious mind, we create a place for the subconscious to emerge.

Through consistent meditation practice, we learn to notice our thoughts without attachment or judgment. This awareness permits us to get insights into the patterns and beliefs that rule our life. We grow attentive to the subtle signals and intuitions that originate from the depths of our subconscious. With time and practice, meditation becomes a tool for discovering the tremendous store of knowledge inside ourselves.

In addition to meditation, visualization is another strong approach for delving into the subconscious mind. Visualization includes utilizing our imagination to generate vivid mental representations of our intended goals. When we imagine with clarity, passion, and emotion, we send strong signals to the subconscious mind, which then starts to match our reality with our pictured aspirations.

Research has demonstrated that visualization may have a tremendous influence on several parts of our life, including athletic performance, goal attainment, and personal growth. Athletes who imagine themselves effectively performing their talents report enhanced performance in their respective sports. Similarly, those who imagine themselves accomplishing their objectives and desires typically find that their aspirations appear more quickly.

To participate in visualization, choose a peaceful and comfortable area where you may relax without interruptions. Close your eyes and construct a mental picture of what you aspire to attain or feel. Visualize the details, colors, textures, and emotions connected with your ideal conclusion. Engage all your senses to make the vision as vivid and genuine as possible.

As you continue to practice visualization, your subconscious mind starts to assimilate these pictures, thoughts, and feelings. This internalization produces a tremendous alignment between your conscious aspirations and your subconscious programming, setting the scene for the manifestation of your objectives.

By combining the techniques of meditation and visualization, you establish a harmonic balance between your conscious and subconscious brains. Meditation clears the road for the subconscious to express its knowledge, while visualization helps you to actively train your brain with powerful thoughts and goals.

Chapter 3: Rewiring Your Belief System

Recognizing Limiting Beliefs

Our values serve as the basis around which we construct our lives. They affect our ideas, impact our emotions, and eventually decide the consequences we experience. However, many of us retain limiting ideas that operate as roadblocks to our success and satisfaction. In this chapter, we will discuss the relevance of our belief system and go into strategies to detect and overcome limiting beliefs.

Beliefs are deeply embedded mental patterns that we believe to be true. They are generally established in infancy by our parenting, cultural conditioning, and prior experiences. Limiting beliefs are those that confine us, producing self-imposed constraints and hurdles that hinder us from attaining our full potential.

These ideas might emerge in numerous aspects of our life. For example, you may have the attitude that you are not clever enough to pursue a specific vocation or that you are undeserving of love and happiness. These self-limiting ideas build a narrative that becomes the lens through which you perceive yourself and your possibilities.

The first step in rewiring your belief system is to become aware of the limiting ideas that live inside your subconscious mind. Take some time for self-reflection and contemplation. Observe the patterns of your thinking and the doubts and concerns that appear when you contemplate following your objectives or moving outside of your comfort zone.

Pay attention to the words you use when you communicate with yourself. Are there repeating negative self-talk patterns that damage your confidence and conviction in your abilities? These thinking patterns frequently reflect the existence of limiting beliefs that need to be addressed.

Overcoming Self-Sabotage and Negative Programming

Once you have recognized your limiting beliefs, it is necessary to question and reframe them. Recognize that beliefs are not absolute facts but rather interpretations and views of reality. They may be modified and replaced with more powerful beliefs that encourage your development and success.

One successful strategy for combating self-sabotage and negative programming is via the use of affirmations. Affirmations are positive words that affirm a desired belief or goal. By repeating affirmations repeatedly, you may rewire your subconscious mind with new powerful ideas.

For example, if you have a limiting thought that you are not deserving of success, you might construct an affirmation such as, "I am worthy of abundant success in all areas of my life." Repeat this affirmation regularly, ideally in a peaceful condition or during your meditation practice. As you constantly reinforce this new thought, it starts to replace the old limiting belief and molds your perspective of yourself and your potential.

Another useful strategy is to seek data that challenges your limiting assumptions. Engage in activities and surround yourself with people who embody the traits and accomplishments you aspire to. By observing others who have overcome comparable problems or accomplished what you seek, you broaden your conviction in what is achievable for yourself.

Additionally, cultivate self-compassion and self-acceptance. Recognize that everyone has limits and defects, and that progress is a process. Embrace the process of testing and removing your limiting beliefs with patience and respect toward yourself.

As you engage on this road of rewiring your belief system, realize that it takes time and persistent work. Be persistent and devoted to the process. The advantages of removing limiting ideas and adopting powerful ones are enormous. You will find increased confidence, resilience, and an enlarged perspective of what is possible in your life.

Chapter 4: The Art of Positive Thinking

Cultivating Optimism and Gratitude

Our ideas have a huge effect on our emotions, actions, and the events we draw into our life. Positive thinking is a strong tool that helps us to harness the energy of optimism and appreciation, influencing our perspective of reality and opening doors to prosperity and pleasure. In this chapter, we will study the skill of positive thinking and the transforming influence it can have on our lives.

good thinking is not about dismissing the presence of problems or difficulties; rather, it is about intentionally choosing to concentrate on the good parts of our life and fostering an optimistic view. By teaching our thoughts to seek the positive, even amid adversity, we build a mentality that is favorable to growth, resilience, and the realization of our aspirations.

One technique to foster good thinking is via the practice of thankfulness. Gratitude is the act of recognizing and appreciating the benefits, great and little, that surround us. When we show thankfulness, we change our focus from what is missing to what is there in our lives. This simple alteration in attitude has a huge influence on our entire well-being and draws more happy events into our reality.

Start by building a thankfulness practice in your everyday life. Set aside a few minutes each day to dwell on the things you are thankful for. It might be as simple as a gorgeous sunset, a helpful companion, or the chance to learn and develop. Write them down in a gratitude diary or voice them loudly. The act of intentionally noticing and appreciating the gifts in your life boosts your positive thinking and elevates your energy.

Another crucial part of positive thinking is the power of affirmations. Affirmations are positive affirmations that proclaim the reality you intend to create. By repeating affirmations repeatedly, you retrain your subconscious mind and match your ideas with your aspirations.

Choose affirmations that represent the wonderful traits, experiences, and outcomes you intend to create in your life. For example, if you seek financial riches, you may repeat affirmations such as, "I am open to receiving limitless abundance in my life" or "I attract prosperity and abundance effortlessly." Repeat these affirmations with conviction and confidence, enabling them to infiltrate your subconscious mind and influence your view of what is possible.

In addition to affirmations, it is vital to watch your self-talk and intentionally replace negative ideas with positive ones. The way we talk to ourselves has a huge influence on our self-image and general mentality. Whenever you discover yourself engaged in self-criticism or negative self-talk, intentionally confront those ideas and rephrase them in a positive and uplifting manner.

Surrounding oneself with happiness and inspiration is also vital for building a good mentality. Seek uplifting novels, podcasts, or inspiring quotations that connect with you. Engage in things that offer you delight and match your interests. Surround yourself with friendly and like-minded persons that inspire and elevate you. The more you immerse yourself in good situations and influences, the more your thinking will be impacted positively.

Remember, positive thinking is not a one-time event but a continuous discipline. It demands constancy, discipline, and self-awareness. It may take time to rewire your thinking and change from a generally pessimistic perspective to one of positivity and optimism. Be patient with yourself and enjoy even the tiniest wins along the road.

By fostering positive thinking, you create a fertile foundation for the manifestation of your wishes and the achievement of your objectives. Positive ideas and emotions have a higher vibrational frequency, attracting matching vibrations into your life. As you match your ideas, beliefs, and emotions with positivity, you become a magnet for prosperity, success, and pleasure.

Chapter 5: Unleashing Creativity through the Subconscious Mind

The Creative Process and the Role of Intuition

Creativity is a tremendous energy that lies inside each of us, ready to be released. It is through the harnessing of our subconscious mind that we may tap into this wellspring of creativity and unleash our intrinsic capacity to think outside the box, solve problems, and bring out novel ideas. In this chapter, we will investigate the importance of the subconscious mind in the creative process and how to develop our creativity and problem-solving skills.

The creative process is a voyage of inquiry, experimenting, and expression. It entails delving into the depths of our subconscious mind, where unique thoughts, connections, and insights lie waiting to be uncovered. The subconscious mind is a reservoir of creativity and intuition, circumventing the constraints of rationality and logical thinking.

To unlock your creativity, it is necessary to establish an atmosphere that fosters and supports your subconscious mind. Find an area that enables you to rest, free from interruptions and external constraints. Engage in activities that foster a state of flow, where your mind may enter a state of heightened attention and absorption.

Imagination is a fundamental factor in the creative process. It is via our imagination that we may transcend the confines of what is known and envisage new possibilities. Engage in activities that engage your imagination, such as brainstorming, fantasizing, or indulging in creative endeavors like sketching, writing, or playing a musical instrument. Allow your imagination to roam, examine alternative views, and consider unexpected thoughts.

Embrace the power of intuition in the creative process. Intuition is the subconscious mind's technique of transmitting its insights and wisdom to our conscious consciousness. It is sometimes defined as a "gut feeling" or a profound understanding that helps us in making choices and finding hidden realities. Cultivate your intuition by paying attention to the subtle nudges, hunches, and intuitive flashes that come inside you. Trust your instincts and allow them to lead you in your creative activities.

Problem-solving is another area where the subconscious mind shines. When presented with difficulty or impediment, tap into your subconscious store of information and experience. Take a step back and let your mind assimilate the information at a subconscious level. Sometimes, the finest ideas arise when we let go of conscious effort and let our subconscious mind work its magic.

To boost problem-solving skills, participate in activities that foster a calm and open state of mind, such as meditation, walks in nature, or indulging in hobbies that offer you delight. These activities provide room for your subconscious mind to assimilate information and generate connections that may have evaded your conscious thinking.

Remember that creativity is a talent that can be cultivated and fostered over time. Be patient with yourself and enjoy the process of discovery and experimenting. Allow yourself to make errors and learn from them. Trust in the knowledge and capacities of your subconscious mind to help you towards unique solutions and breakthrough ideas.

Chapter 6: Harnessing the Subconscious for Goal Achievement

Setting Clear and Empowering Goals

The power of the subconscious mind may be exploited to push us toward the attainment of our objectives. However, to successfully employ this ability, it is vital to create clear and powerful objectives that connect with both our conscious and subconscious minds. In this chapter, we will discuss the process of defining goals that correspond with the subconscious mind and ways for merging conscious and subconscious efforts toward goal attainment.

Setting clear and defined objectives is key for properly engaging the subconscious mind. Vague or unclear objectives make it hard for the subconscious to understand and strive towards. When defining objectives, be as explicit as possible about what you want to accomplish. Define your objectives in terms of quantifiable results, timelines, and the activities necessary to reach them.

Additionally, it is crucial to link your objectives with your beliefs and interests. Goals that are following your basic beliefs and personal aspirations provide a feeling of purpose and drive that connect strongly with your subconscious mind. Take the time to focus on what is important to you and ensure that your objectives are aligned with your true self.

Empowering objectives extend your skills and fire your excitement. While it is vital to make objectives that are practical and achievable, it is as important to set goals that challenge and inspire you. Your subconscious mind thrives on development and expansion, and powerful objectives inspire a feeling of excitement and possibilities.

Aligning Conscious and Subconscious Efforts

To harness the power of the subconscious mind for goal attainment, it is vital to synchronize your conscious and subconscious efforts. The conscious mind establishes the goal, formulates the strategy, and conducts purposeful acts, while the subconscious mind gives the underlying support and direction.

One powerful strategy for synchronizing conscious and subconscious efforts is visualization. Create a vivid mental picture of yourself already having attained your objective. Visualize the details, feelings, and sensations connected with your desired goal. Engage all your senses to make the vision as vivid and genuine as possible. This approach conveys your objectives to the subconscious mind and activates its creative problem-solving talents to help you create them.

More to imagery, affirmations play a significant role in synchronizing conscious and subconscious efforts. Craft positive affirmations that confirm your conviction in the attainment of your objectives. Repeat these affirmations with conviction and persistence, enabling them to reach your subconscious mind and strengthen powerful ideas.

Another approach to merge conscious and subconscious efforts is to leverage the power of emotions. Emotions are the language of the subconscious mind, and when matched with your objectives, they become potent catalysts for manifestation. Generate positive feelings such as appreciation, excitement, and delight while you think about your objectives. Embody the feelings associated with already having attained your intended results, and use these emotions to influence your actions and choices.

Regularly examine your objectives and progress to keep them at the forefront of your conscious and subconscious thinking. This continual conscious awareness helps to sustain concentration and momentum toward goal attainment. Celebrate even the slightest triumphs along the road, since this strengthens good connections and indicates to your subconscious mind that you are making progress.

Remember that the subconscious mind acts beyond the domain of time and space. Trust in its capacity to function in the background, even when you are not actively thinking about your objectives. Stay open to intuitive insights, synchronicities, and opportunities that may come, since these are frequently signals that your subconscious mind is aligning events to support your objectives.

As you blend conscious and subconscious efforts toward goal attainment, you tap into the tremendous pool of resources, creativity, and guidance that lives inside you. By creating clear and powerful objectives and connecting your conscious and subconscious mind, you release the full potential of your subconscious mind to materialize your greatest wants and build a life of satisfaction and success.

Chapter 7: Healing and Transformation

The subconscious mind contains great potential not just for goal success but also for healing emotional scars and fostering significant change. In this chapter, we will examine how to tap into the power of the subconscious mind to heal previous traumas, remove emotional baggage, and generate permanent good change in our lives.

Emotional scars and traumas from the past may frequently limit our personal progress and well-being. These unresolved events may surface as negative thinking patterns, self-limiting beliefs, and harmful actions. However, by working with the subconscious mind, we may address these wounds at their base and create the road for healing and change.

One effective way for mending emotional scars is via guided imagery and visualization. By accessing the subconscious mind's images and symbolic language, we may journey through prior events and reinterpret them in a manner that supports healing and development. Guided by a qualified expert or via self-guided practice, these visualizations assist us to release imprisoned emotions, obtain insights, and construct new powerful narratives.

Affirmations also play a crucial part in mending emotional scars. By actively constructing positive affirmations that challenge negative ideas and self-perceptions, we may rewire the subconscious mind and replace old wounds with new empowered beliefs. Consistent repeating of these affirmations helps to cement them into the subconscious, eventually transforming our perspective of ourselves and the world.

Forgiveness is another vital part of healing and growth. By developing forgiveness, both towards ourselves and others, we remove the emotional baggage that weighs us down and hamper our growth. The subconscious mind may be a tremendous ally in the process of forgiving. Through guided meditations, affirmations, and visualization exercises, we may tap into the well of compassion and understanding inside ourselves, enabling forgiveness to flow organically.

Creating Lasting Positive Change

The subconscious mind holds the key to creating lasting good impact on our life. It is via this sphere that our profoundly established behaviors, beliefs, and patterns are stored. By working with the subconscious, we may reprogram these patterns, replacing old behaviors with new, empowered ones.

One powerful way for producing good transformation is via self-hypnosis or hypnotherapy. These methods include producing a calm state of mind, known as a trance when the subconscious mind becomes extremely receptive to ideas and affirmations. Under the supervision of a skilled expert or via self-hypnosis techniques, we may rewire our subconscious programming, opening the path for sustainable beneficial transformation.

Another important strategy for producing change is the use of positive imagery. By vividly visualizing oneself engaged in desirable activities and experiencing favorable results, we encourage our subconscious mind to match our ideas, beliefs, and actions with our vision. Visualization helps to develop a strong neural pathway in the brain, making it simpler to actualize our intended changes.

Consistency and repetition are crucial variables in producing permanent good change. By continuously exercising new behaviors, we reinforce the new neural connections in our brains, making them stronger and more automatic over time. It is crucial to incorporate these new habits into our everyday life and commit to them with devotion and effort.

Additionally, building a supportive atmosphere is vital for maintaining good change. Surround yourself with people who elevate and encourage you, and participate in activities that reinforce your intended improvements. Seek materials, such as books, podcasts, or seminars, that give assistance and inspiration throughout your transformative path.

Self-reflection and introspection are crucial disciplines when it comes to establishing permanent good change. Take the time to examine your inner landscape, discover any underlying beliefs or anxieties that may be holding you back, and confront them with compassion and understanding. Journaling, meditation, or counseling may be useful tools in this process, helping you to achieve insight and remove any emotional barriers that inhibit your development.

Lastly, recognize your victories, no matter how tiny they may appear. Acknowledge the progress you have achieved and the beneficial improvements you have adopted in your life. By celebrating your triumphs, you reinforce positive connections in your subconscious mind, further reinforcing the new patterns and habits you have established.

Through the power of the subconscious mind, healing and change become possible and sustained. By engaging with the subconscious, we may heal old hurts, discharge emotional baggage, and generate permanent good change in our lives. It is a path of self-discovery, self-compassion, and self-empowerment that leads to a deep change in our being.

Conclusion: Living a Life Aligned with the Power Within

As we approach the end of our journey into the power of the subconscious mind, it is evident that we contain an incredible amount of potential inside us. The subconscious mind, with its untapped resources and powerful impact, holds the key to unlocking our real talents and living a life aligned with our innermost wishes and ambitions. Throughout this book, we have studied the numerous components of the subconscious mind and experienced its enormous effect on goal accomplishment, creativity, healing, and change.

We have learned that the subconscious mind acts outside the sphere of our conscious consciousness, affecting our ideas, beliefs, and actions in ways we may not completely grasp. It is through our awareness and active involvement with the subconscious that we may harness its power and utilize it to actualize our aspirations.

In the world of goal attainment, we have discovered that by defining clear and powerful objectives, connecting our conscious and subconscious efforts, and applying visualization, affirmations, and emotional alignment, we may drive ourselves toward success and satisfaction. The subconscious mind becomes our constant partner, working relentlessly to materialize our innermost aspirations.

In examining the power of the subconscious in creativity, we have tapped into the wellspring of imagination, intuition, and problem-solving talents that reside inside us. By fostering our creativity, allowing ourselves to think beyond the box, and relying upon the insights and inspiration that spring from our subconscious, we become catalysts for innovation and uniqueness.

We have also experienced the remarkable healing and change that happens when we engage the power of the subconscious mind. By working through old traumas, releasing emotional baggage, and practicing forgiveness and self-compassion, we prepare the path for personal development and substantial transformations in our lives. Through methods such as guided imagery, affirmations, self-hypnosis, and visualization, we may reprogram our subconscious habits and produce permanent good change.

As we complete this book, it is vital to remember that our journey with the subconscious mind is continuous. It is a lifetime collaboration, a dance between our conscious and subconscious selves, continually changing and deepening as we continue to investigate and extend our awareness.

Living a life aligned with the power within involves dedication, self-reflection, and a willingness to accept the unknown. It asks for an unflinching conviction in our innate potential and a devotion to fostering our connection with the subconscious mind. It is a voyage of self-discovery, self-mastery, and self-empowerment.

With the information and insights obtained through this investigation, we are ready to explore the wide territory of our subconscious mind and unlock its full potential. Let us start on this magnificent voyage with open hearts and minds, embracing the chances for development, creativity, healing, and change that lie before us.

May your adventure with the power of the subconscious mind be one of deep self-discovery, infinite potential, and the realization of your greatest ambitions. Embrace the power inside you and build a life that is a real representation of your actual self. The moment has arrived to step into your greatness and live a life connected with the power inside.